Isabel Renner

Wyld Woman

developed with Cameron King

Salamander Street

PLAYS

First published in 2025 by Salamander Street Ltd., a Wordville imprint. (info@salamanderstreetcom).

Wyld Woman, Isabel Renner, 2025

Cover image by Ben Blaustein.

PB ISBN: 9781068233463

10 9 8 7 6 5 4 3 2 1

Further copies of this publication can be purchased from www.salamanderstreet.com

Wordville

For Jeri

ACKNOWLEDGEMENTS

Cameron King for your genius mind and generous soul—thank you for creating this with me.

Catherine Schreiber for believing in us, guiding the way, and making a Shy Girl's dream come true—all while having too much fun.

Jeri Slater for your boundless heart, Ray Gaspard for your magic sparkle, Sheer Figman for your brilliance and care, Shaunie Lewis for protecting the vibe, Robin Aren for laying the joyous egg of this journey.

Clara Gamsu, Julian Manjerico, Chad Pierre Vann (+Jug) for being there for every single early iteration. I will always see you when I perform.

Delia and Niall Cunningham for your inspiration and support.

Rebecca Gwyther for being the British woman I hope to one day become.

The ultimate group of Legends: Stephanie Moore and Jennifer Thomas at United Agents, Brett Goldstein, Becca McGreevy, Carter Amaden, Jenny Kleiman, Don Roy King, Kate King, Breakfast, Peter Carroll, Jackie, Gus Mahoney, Maia Karo, Noga Meron Karo, Bridgit Dengel Gaspard, Izzy Koko, Walter Sorel, Rebecca Mitzner, Sasha Cnishchuk, Sofi Duemichen, Laura Cahill, Andrea Schiavoni, David Switzer, Andrew Patino, Zeke St. John, Heather Rasche, Alison Ho, Megan Mook, Ina Grix, Nathan and Maeve from Assembly, Maeve Press, Sarina Freda, Calum Mowatt, Tegu Hoffman, Meechee Miller, Pino, Nigel Miles-Thomas, Nigel Berkeley.

Daniel for making the world feel like a glance across a Downton Abbey dinner table.

Matisse and Khandis, Aggie and Kaelan for showing me the meaning of True Love.

Charlie for your jazz pants, Bearcub for being my best friend.

Mom for showing me how beautiful it is to be a Shy Girl.

Naj for, oh my God, just everything.

Gabs and Louie for your notes, feedback and tough love.

Wyld Woman: The Legend of Shy Girl was first performed at Southwark Playhouse, London, opening on Friday 24 October 2025.

CAST

Shy Girl	**Isabel Renner**

COMPANY

Writer	**Isabel Renner**
Director	**Cameron King**
Producer	**Catherine Schreiber**
Set & Costume Designer	**Lucy Fowler**
Lighting Designer	**Catja Hamilton**
Sound Designer	**Sasha Howe**
General Manager	**RJG Productions**
Production Manager	**Charlie Rayner**
Rehearsal Stage Manager	**Carter Amaden**
Stage Manager	**April Johnston**
Associate Production Manager	**Liam Clark**
Artwork	**Ben Blaustein**

With thanks to Content Bestie, Becca Pratt, Mobius PR, Southwark Playhouse, Erin Pearlman, Jaime Vallés and The Drama League.

In 2024, *Wyld Woman: The Legend of Shy Girl* received a development production at Edinburgh Festival Fringe, produced by Sheer Figman, Ray Gaspard and Jeri Slater.

THE CAST AND CREATIVES

Isabel Renner | Performer & Playwright

Isabel Renner is a writer, performer and aspiring saxophonist from New York City. She performed *Wyld Woman* at the Southwark Playhouse in Autumn of 2025, after a run at the Edinburgh Fringe Festival in 2024. She has appeared on screen in *Blue Bloods* (CBS), as well as on stage at Shakespeare's Globe, Vineyard Theatre, Ensemble Studio Theatre and Fault Line Theatre.

Cameron King | Director

Cameron King is a native New Yorker and former child who works with a strong base in play and collaborative freedom. Directing credits include: *1 in a Chameleon* (Loft 393), *¿baby blue?* (Ars Nova), *Rent* (Southern Plains Productions), *Indian Summer* (Bay Street Theater), *Butchery Lessons* (The Tank), *When We Were Young and Unafraid* (East Village Basement), *Wyld Woman: The Legend of Shy Girl* (Edinburgh Fringe), and *Clue: On Stage* (Timberlake Playhouse). Cameron is thrilled to be making her London directing debut with the team at Southwark Playhouse. LaGuardia Drama Alum. BFA: Carnegie Mellon.

Catherine Schreiber | Producer

Five-time Tony and Olivier Award-winning producer. London productions include: *Burlesque, The Lion, the Witch, and the Wardrobe, Company, The Scottsboro Boys, Dreamgirls* and *The King's Speech*. Broadway Productions Include: *Cabaret at the Kit Kat Club, The Lehman Trilogy, The Roommate, A Christmas Carol, The Play that Goes Wrong, Life of Pi,* and *Peter Pan Goes Wrong*. Tony-winning shows include: *Company, The Lehman Trilogy, The Inheritance, Angels in America* and *Clybourne Park*. Her 11 Tony nominations include: *Cabaret, The Sign in Sidney Brustein's Window, Death of a Salesman, Peter and the Starcatcher, Fiddler on the Roof, The Scottsboro Boys* and *Next Fall*. She won the Olivier for *Company*, and the five nominations include: *The Scottsboro Boys, Dreamgirls, Show Boat,* and *People, Places and Things*. Winner of the Offies Award for *The Life,* starring Sharon D. Clarke, at the Southwark Playhouse. She is most proud of bringing *The Scottsboro Boys* to London, which was nominated for 7 Oliviers (over 2 years) and won The Evening Standard Award and the London Critics' Circle Award. Catherine was the winner of the Broadway Global Producer of the Year Award in 2017.

Lucy Fowler | Set & Costume Designer

Lucy trained at The Royal Welsh College of Music and Drama, studying Design for Performance. Theatre Credits include:

As Set and Costume designer: *Twelfth Night* (Tabard Theatre, Chronicle Theatre Company), *As You Like it* (East London Shakespeare Festival), *Napoleon* (Jermyn Street Theatre), *The Sorcerer* (Wilton's Music Hall and Tour, Charles Court Opera), *Beyond the Fog* (Orange Tree Theatre), *Maladies* (Orange Tree Theatre), *Snow Queen* (Grays Arts Centre and Tour, Arts Outburst Theatre company), *Medea* (Barn Theatre, Rose Bruford College), *Macbeth* and *Romeo and Juliet* (Guildford Shakespeare Company schools Tour and Orange Tree Theatre), *Idomeneo* (Normansfield Theatre, Rose Opera Company), *The things I say when I don't say I love you* (Studio at the Lowry Theatre and Tour, Sam Brady Ltd), *Hush* (Bute Theatre Cardiff and Gate Theatre London, Richard Burton Company.)

As Costume Designer: *A Pissedmas Carol* (Edinburgh Fringe and Leicester Square Theatre, Sh!tfaced Showtime), *The Actress, The Giant Killers, Arty's Ani-Magination* (Edinburgh Fringe Venues, Long Lane Theatre Company), *Carrie* (Trinity Laban conservatoire of Music and Dance.)

As Associate Set and Costume Designer: *The Magic Flute* (Wilton's Music Hall, Charles Court Opera), *As long as we are breathing* (Arcola Theatre), *The Oyster Problem* (Jermyn Street Theatre.)

As Associate Set designer: *Footloose* (Trinity Laban conservatoire of Music and Dance), *Deer Hunt* (Richard Burton Theatre.)

As Associate Costume Designer: *The Lesson* (Southwark Playhouse, Icarus theatre company.)

Lucy also worked as freelance Assistant designer at the Royal Shakespeare company and is frequently Assistant designer for Set and Costume Designer's Nicky Shaw, Stewart J Charlesworth and Zahra Mansouri.

Catja Hamilton | Lighting Designer

Catja is a Lighting Designer working primarily in theatre and opera, who particularly enjoys working on new writing. She is a former Creative Associate of Jermyn Street Theatre and Resident Designer at NDT Broadgate. Catja is also a Co-Director of Airlock Theatre.

Previous credits include: *1:17am* (Theatre503); *Handel's Semele* (Waterperry Opera Festival); *Ugly Sisters* (Soho Theatre); *Fiddler on the Roof* (UK Tour, Associate to Aideen Malone); *King of Pangea* (King's Head Theatre); *Puppy* (King's Head Theatre); *Oh My Pain, My Beautiful Pain!* (Pleasance Theatre); *Acid's Reign* (Pleasance Theatre); *The Maids* (Jermyn Street Theatre), *I Didn't Know I Was Polish* (Voila Theatre Festival), *Utoya* (Arcola Theatre), *The Turn of the Screw* (Waterperry Opera Festival), *The Mosinee Project* (New Diorama Theatre and Edinburgh Fringe), *Talawa Firsts on Tour* (Talawa Studio & UK tour), *Pansexual Pregnant Piracy* (Soho Theatre), *Scarlet Sunday* (Omnibus Theatre), *The Pursuit of Joy* (Jermyn Street Theatre), *The Wolf, The Duck, and The Mouse* (Unicorn Theatre), *Passing* (Park Theatre), *Rip Van Winkle* (Hoxton Hall), *The Importance of Being... Earnest?* (UK tour), *Sorry We Didn't Die At Sea* (Park Theatre), *Birthright* (Finborough Theatre), *Agrippina* (Jackson's Lane), *The Oyster Problem* (Jermyn Street Theatre), *SNAIL* (VAULT Festival), *Acid's Reign* (VAULT Festival), *Lesbian Space Crime* (Soho Theatre), *Cassandra* (UK tour), *Time and Tide* (UK tour), *Another America* (Park Theatre), *Paradise Lost* (The Shipwright), *The Anarchist* (Jermyn Street Theatre), *An Intervention* (Riverside Studios), *Lizard King* (UK tour), *The 4th Country* (Park Theatre).

Sasha Howe | Sound Designer

Sasha Howe is a London-based sound designer, engineer and composer with experience across theatre, games, and live events. A graduate of the Royal Central School of Speech and Drama, Sasha has worked on productions like *Speed* and *Elvis*, and is currently Head of Sound for a video game project while freelancing at major UK venues.

Catherine Schreiber presents

Wyld Woman:
The Legend of Shy Girl

by Isabel Renner

developed with Cameron King

CHARACTERS

SHY GIRL

young female New Yorker

NOTES ON PRODUCTION

All characters are played by the same actor. SHY GIRL's lines are in "inverted commas" when speaking in a remembered scene with other characters.

In the opening and closing, SIRI and SHELLY, the therapist, are pre-recorded.

Everything else is performed live.

PRESHOW

A full-fledged legend rave. Party lights. Loud girlypop music with a few 'My Fair Lady' remixes peppered in (perhaps a The Rain in Spain//Party in the USA mashup?)

'HEY LEGENDS, WELCOME TO MY APARTMENT' is projected in shaky handwriting on the back wall of a cramped, but festively decorated New York City apartment.

As they enter, each audience member is given a name tag to which SHY GIRL can refer throughout the show. A couple of audience members are seated on stage at the dining table. One audience member in the front row should be given a stack of SHY GIRL's index cards.

Lights and projection fade out. In the blackout, we hear a recording:

SHY GIRL VOICEOVER: Hey legends
Welcome to Wyld Woman.

BWOOOM. An epic, Wrestlemania-style underscoring bursts into the space.

The Legend of Shy Girl.

BWOOOM.

Oh my God wait
Should I say 'Legend of Shy Girl'?
Okay
Let me start over

Hey legends.

BWOOOM.

Welcome to Wyld Woman.

BWOOOM.

I'm Buddy. I'm the boss.

Oh sh*t that's the cake boss intro

BWOOOM. The music begins to climax.

Okay
Let's get this party started in 5, 4, 3, 2...

The epic music builds and builds and builds into a grand finish. Lights up.

On stage is SHY GIRL, blinded by stage lights and terrified of the audience. She reaches for her phone.

OPENING

SHY GIRL: Siri
Call Shelly

SIRI: Which Shelly would you like me to call?

SHY GIRL: Shelly
the therapist

SIRI: Calling Shelly the therapist

Sound of the phone dialing.

SHELLY: Hiiiii!

SHY GIRL: Hi Shelly
It's me

SHELLY: I know
I have your contact saved!

SHY GIRL: Oh
Sorry

SHELLY: No sorries, puppy cat

SHY GIRL: Oh yeah, okay
Listen
I'm really nervous
I don't think I can do this

SHELLY: Aww yes you can

SHY GIRL: No, I can't

SHELLY: YES. YOU. CAN
They're gonna love you

SHY GIRL: Mm
Fair enough

SHELLY: 'Member, lovebug.
Don't be afraid to be a lil' vulnerable
You gotta open up if you want real human connection

SHY GIRL: Uh huh

SHELLY: And don't forget!
    It never hurts
    To practice some of those talking points!

SHY GIRL: Yeah Shelly
    That's what I was about to do

SHY GIRL places her phone down.

She approaches the audience in terror and confusion.

She stands awkwardly for a few moments before it is made clear...
She has forgotten what to say.

SHY GIRL: Umm...
    I forgot
    Does anyone have the prompts?

The audience member with the index card, hopefully, offers them to her.

Oh thank you, [name of audience member]

SHY GIRL checks the first index card.

Hey legends

...

Welcome to my apartment

'HEY LEGENDS. WELCOME TO MY APARTMENT.' is projected on the back wall.

She flips to the next index card: 'REQUEST SHOES OFF.'

Would you please take your shoes off?
My roommate just waxed

Oh yeah, Okay
You don't have to
Sorry

Next index card: 'YOU HAVE TO OPEN UP IF YOU WANT REAL HUMAN CONNECTION.'

SHY GIRL: What's up?
Oh God
This is awkward
For me
Not you
You're really awesome
I just...
I can be a little shy sometimes

And yeah, [name of audience member], I totally agree
Shy can be cute
But for me I wouldn't classify it as the cute kind
I would say it's more the kind that's like
You're confused as to where to go to
Learn how to have a conversation with another person your age
And your hands kind of shake when people look at you
And your most romantic memory
Is actually just a scene from *My Fair Lady*
That you watch quite regularly

'On the Street Where You Live' begins to play. It's kind of awkward. But SHY GIRL is moved.

SHY GIRL: Oh wow

...

So basically I pretend that this
Like British hottie from 1912 and I
Just had the most tender evening imaginable
And that he's singing this song about me
And yeah that's
That's how I get my love needs met

Okay
That's plenty

Music ends.

Anyways...

What was I saying
Oh yeah I'm totally shy
And when you're shy like me
Things are just a little harder
And I'm talking basic things

Like I guess
I'm not that good at making friends
And I live here in New York City
Which means I see groups of legends everywhere I look

And—oh and by legends
I just mean cool people
You know maybe
Smoking cigarettes
Having tattoos
Being sexually fulfilled

Like someone like you, [name of legend in the audience]

Yeah
Legends
Are literally my idols

And it sucks cuz
I can't just go up to them
And be like
"Hey legends, can I play?"
So that's a bust

But no
Don't be ridiculous, [name of audience member]
I have my people

Like I share this apartment
With what you might call a hot girl roommate
And we're friends, Memphis and I
—that's the hot girl's name
It's such an amazing name—
We're friends
Cuz we live together

But actually to be honest...

Most nights I do try to 'go to bed'
Before she gets home from work
—which is like 5:30-6 O'CLOCK—
So depending on the season
The sun is often still out by the time
I'm cozied up in my quarters with the door closed

MEMPHIS

SHY GIRL: But I'm not... weird
You know? It's not...
And I don't always get the timing right

Even a few days ago
I'm eating dinner at 4:30PM
That's my dinner time
That's before Memphis is supposed to get home

And mid-bite
The front door swings open

And I get all weird cuz
I don't really like when people watch me eat
But Memphis doesn't seem to notice my discomfort

SHY GIRL's stiffness suddenly melts into sorority girl sex appeal as she leans across the kitchen counter and becomes MEMPHIS.

MEMPHIS: Mm what's cooking, Mamacita!

SHY GIRL: Oh yeah I should mention
Memphis has adopted a lisp in recent months
Because apparently she's in her 'femme fatale era'
And wants to 'dominate men'?
So a lisp has something to do with that
I'm a little hazy on the exact logic

Anyways
She sits down with me
She looks me over
I kinda squirm

MEMPHIS: You look cute...
A little oily
Like salad dressing
But wait
I love salad

SHY GIRL: "Oh. Thanks?"

MEMPHIS: You're welcome

   ...

   Omigod I just thought of something so funny

MEMPHIS laughs performatively.

SHY GIRL: "Um
   What did you think of?"

MEMPHIS: Ughh fine I'll bite
   So Jeff
   My Tinder date from last night
   —I know, right, it's like why is that his name
   I can't—
   Emm
   Out of nowhere he literally says to me
   I've never met a woman like you before
   And I was like, Jeff
   Stop! It's not a competition
   Like I'm a girl's girl are you kidding?
   But at the same time
   I did kind of know what he meant by that
   Like I'm not your run of the mill basic bitch
   I mean
   I'm soulful
   I'm mysterious
   I'm poetic
   Like move aside, Rupi Kaur
   I am milk and I am honey
   I mean right bubba?
   You know me

SHY GIRL: "Yeahhh,
   Yeah yeah, totally
   Y-you are"

MEMPHIS: Aww thanks
   Anywhom
   Jeff is coming over tonight for his second helping
   We'll be having tons of sex
   So wear your earplugs bubba

And T God because I'm sorrrrr horny
—Omigod the Australian accent is all over TikTok
And I'm like
This is my humor
Like wait I've found my giggle tribe
Like it's obscure but we out here fam—

But waiiiit what about you lovie?
You never open up
Always so quiet, so sheltered
Like rahhh
Tell me things oh please, oh please

SHY GIRL: "Ohhh...
    Eh
    N
    I—
    Oh
    n"

You know like shy stuff
Thankfully Memphis is quickly onto the next thought

MEMPHIS: Omigod, bub
You're gonna pee
I bought Jeff an apron for tonight
Because I wanna do muffin man role-play
Like I wanna make him cum down Drury lane
Okay ahhhh (*baby scream*)
I gotta go wax

MEMPHIS twirls off.

SHY GIRL: And yeah that's typically how our conversations go
Like I don't always know how to respond
But the good thing about Memphis
Is she doesn't need you to respond

Which is kind of the beauty of our friendship
Like I'm a really good listener
Memphis is a really good talker

She's actually in the other room having s-e-x right now
So you may hear her from time to time

But yeah... we're like so close
So totally
I have my people

And I also have a bunch of imaginary friends
Who are literally my soul mates
So I'm not lonely luckily... but yeah

Awkward. Next index card.

SHY GIRL: Upside down
Umm let's see

She flips it over.

CHEZ MAXENCE

SHY GIRL: Oh!
That's easy enough

Index card: 'WHAT DO YOU GUYS DO FOR WORK?'

What do you guys do for work?

No response.

Cool!
Me?
Oh I work at Chez Maxence
Which, [name of audience member] I know you know
I saw you there last week

But like for those who don't
It's a really fancy restaurant
And randomly a hotspot for British celebrities
Dame Judi Dench
Famous rockstars
They all come when they're visiting New York
And that's awesome
Cuz I'm a total anglophile

But at Chez Maxence I'm just a server
And I LOVE working there
I guess not love
I guess it kinda sucks

Cuz I don't have any work friends
And I get pretty shy around the famous British patrons
And my manager Patrice
Kind of hates me
Because of my shyness

Like just last Saturday
I'm working the brunch shift
Just doing my thing
When suddenly Patrice summons me into the back office

"What am I doing here?"

SHY GIRL leans on the dining room table and swishes around a glass of wine, becoming PATRICE, a middle-aged woman of infinite rage and neurosis.

PATRICE: What are you doing here
You tell me
I sure as hell don't know

SHY GIRL: "Oh I uh—"

PATRICE: *(mocking)* 'Oh I uh'
Sweetheart
This the third time this month
I have a customer come up to me
Ask me why their server
—Meaning you—
Is so fucking quiet

SHY GIRL: "I'm sorry"

PATRICE: Don't say sorry
That'll really piss me off

No it's ridiculous
I ask a simple thing
You go up
List the specials
Somewhat audibly

You know
I'm not asking you to belt it
I'm not asking you to do a whole Cynthia Erivo
I mean a two-day-old Amish mouse
Would have more bravado than you

And the worst part is
You want to know which customer it was this time?

SHY GIRL: "Which customer was it this time?"

PATRICE: David Attenborough
Just David fuckin' Attenborough

Guess we won't be seeing him back at Chez motherfucking
Maxence anytime soon
Fuck me up the ass

SHY GIRL: Okay
Context
A lot of the dishes at Chez Maxence are French
And I don't speak French
So I get really shy about saying those words

You know
I'll be like
"Today's special side dishes are
(French mumbling) un lemi de lu supra deux trois ohhh ee I
louis the fourteenth"
You know like shy stuff

And then the customer
—David Attenborough in this case—
Will just order off the menu cuz he can't really hear me

It's not that big of a deal
But I guess it is to Patrice

PATRICE: Do you know because of you
David Attenborough missed out on our petits pois a la
française

(Furious chortle)

Like wh?
Like you can't make that shit up

I mean
It's ridiculous
I'm humiliated
I'm having a panic attack
I need a Xanax
I need a Xanax right now

And also one of those SSRIs that kill your sex drive
Cuz my God does David pop my rocks off
Say that three times fast

SHY GIRL: "My God does David pop my rocks off"

PATRICE: No oh, my God, don't actually
No just go
Back to work
Now
Please
I mean I have half a mind to fire you right the fuck now
But by some act of God
I was not born a supreme fucking cunt

PATRICE squeezes her wine glass and we hear the sound of glass shattering.

SHY GIRL: So I go cry in the bathroom
Not because I care
I just get really emotional when people are mean to me?
I'm funny that way

SHY GIRL checks the next index card: 'WHO WAS YOUR FIRST LOVE?'

A burst of impish glee.

But like
Don't feel bad for me
Like Patrice is fine
And honestly...
She isn't even the awkwardest part of work

PINO

SHY GIRL: The awkwardest part
   Is actually this human called Pino
   —a server like myself—
   Who I was actually
   Romantically AND sexually involved with
   For... for a time

   You see
   I'm something of a late bloomer
   But at the time I like
   Really wanted to bloom with Pino

   And Pino is...
   How to describe Pino...?
   Pino is like
   The human version of...
   A 2005 desktop Dell

   You know?
   He loves Reddit...
   He's been known to wear his retainer to work on occasion...
   He says things like...

SHY GIRL mimes rolling napkins robotically as PINO.

Mii music underscores.

PINO: I'm one of those guys
   Who's uh
   Real passionate about personal development
   And kinda biohacking my brain to optimize my
   More or less never ending stream of creativity
   As I like to say uh
   Ted talks are my drug of choice

PINO makes finger guns like the sex pistol he is.

Mii music fades.

SHY GIRL: Yeah
Stuff like that!

And
Well
I'm a romantic—

'On the Street Where You Live' begins to play again.

—Like this is my anthem

And right before Pino and I
Started seeing each other
I was feeling a little bereft of a man's love

Song fadeth.

You know
My hot roommate Memphis has had thousands of
boyfriends
In the span of time that we've lived together
I on the other hand
Have had I guess like... *(calculating)* negative thousand
boyfriends?

And she's always coming up to me in the apartment
going—

MEMPHIS: Bubba?
Hi!
Hi hi
Right here
Emm
I wanna find you someone
I wanna help

SHY GIRL: And you know then she puts her hand on her heart
Like she's gonna perform a miracle

And I'm like
"Oh I'm fine Memphis
I don't need anyone"

But like of course I need someone
Of course I crave a man's love

Because a man's love is something sturdy and unchanging
Unto which you can affix your entire life
And never again have to have a care in the world
A man's love would set me free

So eventually I follow Memphis' lead
I create a Tinder profile
I set my preferences to bad boys only
Because Memphis tells me
'Bad boys will make allowances for girls in their awkward
era?'

And of course
I've had tons of imaginary lovers
(gestures to an Imaginary Lover in the audience)
—that guy from *My Fair Lady* being my latest paramour—
And those relationships are deeply fulfilling
At a certain point you get a little hungry
For real human connection

And then there was Pino...
Working at Chez Maxence
I didn't really pay him any mind
Cuz even I'm not above ignoring randoms

And if the desktop Dell analogy didn't make it clear
Pino is not a bad boy
Nor is he a British man with a voice like butter

But one strange Autumn day...
Pino comes up to me in the Chez Maxence kitchen
And hands me a plate

Mii music.

PINO: Hey
    I'm gonna need you to take this to table 18 for me
    Me stomach hurts and I gotta use the bathroom
    I think it might be diarrhea

SHY GIRL: And so I say "sure"
    And in the midst of the plate transference
    Our hands touch

Mü music fades into 'On the Street Where You Live.' SHY GIRL suddenly and delightedly realizes that she's in love.

And I'm suddenly thinking
Okay I don't know where this guy is from
But his robot accent is kinda hot
... And it hits me

A shy little lamb like myself
Isn't supposed to end up with a bad boy!
I need someone nice
Like Pino

I mean
I know I don't know him at this point
But I assume he's nice
Because if you're not cool
You kinda have to be nice if you want to get by in life
That's federal law

Anyways
I'm walking the dish to table 18
Little fireworks of love and desire are busting within me
While Pino diarrheas in the employee bathroom

Like oh my God
He could actually be my boyfriend!
He's not too cool for a life choice like that
But how on earth do I go about making it happen?

'On the Street Where You Live' fades. SHY GIRL propels herself violently across the stage.

I'm propelled violently through flashbacks of my entire life thus far
Why have things never worked out with a guy before?
"Ummm probably because you have shy person issues, bitch"

The tone of my inner critic is harsh
But I know the truth when I hear it

So I spend the next few days kinda contemplating
How does one stop being a shy loser and achieve true love?

THERAPY

SHY GIRL: And try as I might
    I can't seem to crack the code by myself
    But luckily I have a really gifted therapist
    Named Shelly
    —Who's actually one of my good friends
    So yeah it's like I told you, [name of audience member]
    I have my people—

    And
    Shelly
    Is a child therapist
    But I don't know
    Adult therapy sounds so serious
    I just need like a fun size amount of help

    So I'm in my weekly session with Shelly
    We're playing with Calico Critters
    Talking about typical therapy stuff

SHY GIRL sits on the kitchen counter and becomes SHELLY, innocent and open-minded.

SHELLY: So tell me a little bit about your childhood puppy cat

SHY GIRL: "Oh
    I
    Uh"

SHELLY: Well, what were you like when you were my age?

SHY GIRL: To be clear,
    I meant child therapist literally
    Shelly just turned 6 last week!
    And yes her mom does pay me for our sessions
    As I am technically her 'babysitter'
    But she's so wise
    She might as well be a licensed mental health professional

    "When I was your age?
    I don't know
    I guess I was kind of rebellious?"

SHELLY: Rawr!
　　Okay alley cat
　　I like it

SHY GIRL: "Oh no
　　Not like that
　　It's just
　　My parents are legends
　　So I rebelled against them by not being a legend
　　And I am still not a legend
　　So yeah"

SHELLY: What's a legend?

SHY GIRL: "Oh just like a really cool person"

SHELLY: Waaah

SHY GIRL: "Yeah like they might have tattoos or cigarettes
　　But mainly it's just someone who does what they want to do
　　And doesn't do what they don't want to do"

SHELLY: And you're not a legend?

SHY GIRL: "Oh God no
　　I do what I don't want to do
　　And don't do what I want to do all the time"

SHELLY: What's something you want to do?

SHY GIRL: "Um stop being so shy"

SHELLY: But shy is cute

SHY GIRL: "Not the kind I have
　　Sorry"

SHELLY: No sorries, puppy cat
　　Nuh uh uh
　　I'm gonna help you with this
　　Let me think

　　The sound of a stomach growling.

　　Oh! Well first
　　It is time for my morning snack
　　Could you get me some string cheese!

SHY GIRL: "Of course!"

SHELLY: Would you like some too?

SHY GIRL: "Oh no thanks
   I don't really like to eat in front of other people"

SHELLY: Wow you really are shy
   Let's build you up
   Like a lil' magna-tile tower of confidence
   How's that sound
   Huh?

SHY GIRL: "Shelly!
   That sounds awesome
   I need a magna-tile tower of confidence
   You see
   I am on a bit of a quest to turn myself
   Into a lady worthy of true love's kiss
   Among other things
   And I think I found a guy that's just loser enough no
   offense
   That he could actually like me back"
   Shelly is over the moon

SHELLY: I'm over the moon!

   You want my advice?
   You gotta take life into your hands
   And pretend it's your very favorite play dough
   Maybe the sparkly kind?
   Waaah I like sparkles too!

   But you gotta take life
   And mold it into the shape of your wildest dreams!
   AKA
   I think you should ask this lucky boy out
   And I think you should tell him
   I love you
   I love you I love you I love you
   Cuz puppy cat
   You have to open up
   If you want real human connection

Uh oh

SHY GIRL: Our session is cut short
When it becomes abundantly clear
That Shelly has had an accident
Just a number one
But still
I gotta be the adult now

But yeah
She gives amazing advice

And I know it's a little weird to think I like like Pino at this point
But I guess I do?
I mean I've never really talked to him
But by now
I've definitely spent the past few days imagining what it would be like
If he got a little handsomer
And I a little beautifuller
And we both randomly were famous
And went on a Mediterranean vacation
Where we ran into everyone who had ever been mean to me
And suddenly I was way cooler than all those people and they were so intimidated by me and they thought I was so powerful and they wanted my approval and they said sorry for being so mean to you, you're the cool one now and also do you want to hang out and I said I don't know I'm kind of busy with all the friends I have and also with being famous and also with being in love with this really handsome guy named Pino

So yeah I do like him

And this session with Shelly
Was so helpful
I'm totally feeling totally ready to mold the play dough of my life into...
I don't know
A less shy shape?

ASKING HIM OUT

SHY GIRL: So...

'The Embassy Waltz' from My Fair Lady begins to play, as SHY GIRL takes next steps across the stage.

My next steps are obvious
I get home
I log onto the Chez Maxence Slack channel
I scroll through the roster of waitstaff
I find Pino's short little name

I notice he's made his slack profile picture
A sepia-toned photo booth shot of himself
Smiling stiffly but earnestly into the camera
I think
Huh
So this is what the 13th-century Italian poets felt
When they'd found their muse

I muster... the courage of a thousand blazing suns
I slack message a simple

"Hi Pino. Any chance ur free tomorrow after work? Want to hang? No problem if not"

I put my phone on airplane mode
And throw it through the fourth wall

She mimes throwing her phone into the audience.

Because sometimes it's nice to rest in the hopeful unknown for a little

When I check
He's responded
"sure"... "period"
You know the period is kinda like
Boom I love you
(ecstatic) I feel like a princess

Tomorrow comes and before work
I pour a bit of my roommate Memphis'
Mango-flavored vodka into my water bottle

Uh oh!
SHE CATCHES ME

"This isn't what it looks like!"
But she doesn't seem to mind

MEMPHIS: Okay we litty in the morning
Yesss bay-bee!
I knew there was a bad bitch inside of you
Let's take a shot together what the fuck

SHY GIRL: So Memphis and I take shots at
8:30 in the morning

I spend the work shift
Doing typical stuff
Like practicing conversations in my head
And a little out loud when no one's looking
"Hey Pino, how's your diarrhea?"
Biting my nails so much
That the bottom of my stomach is literally lined with
prickly little shards
And taking secret swigs of vodka
So I can be confident
And not scare Pino away with any socially awkward vibes

And suddenly

Lights shift. Perhaps a microphone drops from the ceiling. Drama.

It's showtime baby

FIRST DATE

SHY GIRL: Pino approaches me as I clock out

PINO: So uh... wanna go to my place?

SHY GIRL: (*shrieking*) "SURE!!!" I say
Playing it cool

We get on the subway

Throughout the following, SHY GIRL and PINO mime riding a subway full of bumps, turns and the occasional squeezer by.

He tells me a little bit about himself

PINO: I'm one of those guys
Who found his calling pretty early on in life
Uh
For me it's writing
It's always been writing

SHY GIRL: "Wow I love writing"

PINO: Yup...
I'm actually workin' on what could just be
My uh
My magnum opus right now
It's essentially a hero's journey
Centered around a guy in his 20s
Who is I guess you could say is kinda
Compounded by genius

SHY GIRL: "Wow that sounds right up my alley"

They transfer to another train.

PINO: Yeah not sure about that
But the neat thing is
It's actually based on
A bunch of my old journal entries
You know
Keeping a detailed record of my days
The observations I make

Finding magic in the mundane
Stuff like that

And I take real pride in how a quiet masterpiece
Has emerged from this seemingly simple praxis
Of disciplined bookkeeping

SHY GIRL: "Totally!
So Pino
Ya watching anything good on TV?"

PINO: Nah
I don't like to fry my brain with that garbage
I tend to keep it high brow with foreign films and the like
Speaking of
You wanna watch one?

SHY GIRL: "A foreign film?
Uh YEAH!"

PINO: Great
How's *(unintelligible French)* Ratatouille?

SHY GIRL: "Did you say Ratatouille?"

PINO: Yeah
It's French

SHY GIRL: So...

'Ratatouille Main Theme' begins to play. SHY GIRL climbs on the dining table, where lucky audience members are seated, of course.

Cut to:
Interior Pino's Bedroom
Me. Pino. Mid-Ratatouille
The sensuous streets of Paris
Rats. Food. This song
Oh my God sorry spoiler alert, [name of audience member]
I know you haven't seen it yet!

We're watching
In silence

Like we have so much chemistry
But awkward moments are inevitable
I mean
Love is hard
And also
At this point the effects of the water-bottle vodka
Have pretty much worn off

So I'm just kinda
Intensely watching Ratatouille
Racking my brain for any impressive quips I can make about
the film
To prove to Pino that I too am a Parisian cinephile

When suddenly...
Without saying a thing
Pino rolls over to me
And place his...
Exquisitely thin lips
Upon mine own

'Ratatouille Main Theme' swells. Profoundly romantic.

Every thought in the universe leaves my mind
Except one...
And it's:
Oh. OK
Dreams really do come true!

I mean
I think he loves me
(to the Heavens) I THINK HE LOVES ME
How did I get so lucky?

Anyways
This goes on for
A minute or two and
Before I can mentally prepare
For I guess
The inevitable progression of a smooch sesh

Pino sticks one of his computer-typer fingers into
What I have since come to know as my vaginal canal

Hard cut. SHY GIRL doubles over in agony.

"Ow. Ow. Ow. Ow. Ow."
Oh God
The pain is... unlordly

But Pino is a total optimist

PINO: Wow, you really like that huh?
    Yup. Checks out.
    I'm uh kinda notorious
    For providing women with
    Pretty intense erotic pleasure
    I guess it's my superpower?

    Like
    Captain Pino
    Reporting for duty
    Heee yah!

PINO lunges upward, robot finger first.

SHY GIRL: *(to the audience)* And he continues to swirl
    His robot finger around for a few seconds
    As though collecting a Covid sample or something
    procedural like that
    Before I have to stop him

PINO: Whoa
    You came quick

SHY GIRL: "Yeahhhhh"

    I'm too shy to say otherwise

PINO: Dang... I knew I was good
    But this is off the charts

    *PINO blows smoke from his finger gun and clicks it into his
    imaginary holster belt.*

SHY GIRL: And I start to fret
    So that's what it feels like
    To have a foreign object
    Inside one's vagina?

I don't know if I mentioned it but
I'm a vegan

...

...

...

I mean virgin!
I always mix those two up!

But yeah this amazing first date with Pino
Leads me to a realization
Which is that
I think my vagina might be broken?
I mean like it hurts to pee for the next few days
And all Pino did was
Generously finger me like the sex avenger he is!

And I'm Googling it
And I'm freaking out

SHY GIRL tornadoes around in a storm of anxious terror.

And now I'm convinced I'm never going to be able to have
sex
And if I can't have sex, how is anyone ever going to love me?
And if nobody loves me, am I just gonna be an awkward
loser for all of eternity?

GYNECOLOGIST

SHY GIRL: And this kind of self-inquiry sends me straight into the office
Of a German gynecologist named Jurgen
—he had the first available appointment—

I'm obviously really nervous
Because everything about myself
Makes me shy
And my vagina is no exception
Believe you me
No exception at all

And Jurgen does not do much to ease my nerves
Because he's... he's very serious

SHY GIRL crosses her arms and looks at a clipboard, becoming JURGEN, who has a thick German accent and a somewhat effeminate demeanor.

JURGEN: What is the reason for visit?

SHY GIRL: "Oh I think my vagina might be broken."

JURGEN: Oh no
Let me check

SHY GIRL: And he examines me with an icy cold speculum

SHY GIRL puts her feet in the stirrups.

"Owwww!
That feels like an evil popsicle"
Jurgen is not amused

JURGEN: That hurt you?

SHY GIRL: "Yeah."

JURGEN: Oh no. Are you virgin?

SHY GIRL: "Yeah?"

JURGEN: Oh no

SHY GIRL: "Oh no no no
    Dr. Jurgen, it's not like that
    I mean I basically have a boyfriend"

JURGEN: Oh
    You basically have boyfriend
    But you not have sex

SHY GIRL: "Well no
    We were about to the other night
    We just got caught up
    Watching our favorite movie"

JURGEN: What movie?

SHY GIRL: "Ratatouille"

JURGEN: Iiichh
    You are virgin

JURGEN, disgusted, removes his gloves, throws them away, and pulls out his prescription pad.

    Listen
    Your vagina does not appear 'broken'
    As you say
    I think you are just squeamish
    Because you are virgin

    Perhaps if you have sex with boyfriend
    Then squeamish goes away

JURGEN hands SHY GIRL the prescription. Sex with Boyfriend rX.

SHY GIRL: Yeah
    Jurgen's so scary
    But he's also kind of an evil genius
    Because it's suddenly so clear to me that
    All of my problems
    —AKA my broken vagina and my shy heart—
    Will melt away like snow
    once I have sex... with Pino
    So
    The obvious remedy is sex... with Pino

33

SECOND DATE

SHY GIRL: (*Irish accent*) And it doesn't end there
Oh sorry
Sometimes my Irish side slips out
I'm 27 per cent lass

But yeah it doesn't end there cuz
Pino wants to hang out again the next weekend
—I guess our first date was a smash hit question mark—

SHY GIRL returns to the dining table, now PINO's bed.

Unfortunately, he again tries to stick one of his robot fingers
inside of me
(to PINO) "STOP!
Um can you skip the finger part
And just go in straight with your
Your penis?
Since... you're... such... an... atomic sex bomb?"

Pino unbuttons his pants and shrugs

PINO: You want me to show you the full scope of my powers
Alright already

PINO pulls down his pants. SHY GIRL covers the eyes of an audience member behind her.

SHY GIRL: HIS PENIS!!!!
Me and [audience member at dining table] don't want to see
that!!!
Let's do it from behind!

SHY GIRL spins around and plants her elbows on the table, preparing to uh... take it from behind. She makes direct eye contact with the audience members at the table for moral support.

And I prepare to be devirginized
In three... two... one...
AHHHHHH..??

You guys
When I tell you...
Pino's penis literally gets stuck
Not even a quarter of the way inside of me
It hurts like a monster truck

Pino is deeply, deeply intuitive
So he can sense my agony
And doesn't want to keep going
But I beg him

"PLEASE FORCE IT IN HARDER
I PROMISE I CAN DO THIS"

Eventually I'm fully crying from the pain and he insists on
stopping

*PINO backs off of the dining table. In the following, we can see his penis,
played, to scale, by interchangeable pinky fingers.*

PINO: I can't
I can't anymore
I can tell you're hurting
And I don't like to hurt people

Also
Can I make something very very clear?
Uh... how to put this?

As something of a writing prodigy
I'm inevitably tuned into the human condition
At a pretty remarkable frequency
And in that vein
I'd like you to know that I'm not looking for anything serious
with
This whole you me thing

Can you turn around and make eye contact with me
So I know that you've uh...
For lack of a better phrase
Understood the assignment?

SHY GIRL is still bent over, facing the dining table audience members.

SHY GIRL: I can't really look him in the eyes
Because I'm trying so hard not to cry
For the second time in one evening

SHY GIRL reassumes a normal stance and moves away from the dining table.

I spend the weekend furiously researching
What it means when a guy says he doesn't want anything serious???
But nobody on the Internet
Seems to understand my specific situation
Which is that like he does want to be with me

He just
Well
It's complicated
I mean
I start imagining Pino during vows at our wedding

FANTASY PINO: (*who is British and literally nothing like Real Life PINO*)
Darling, you know I always wanted something serious

SHY GIRL: Oh yeah
Pino is British in my fantasies
Sue me

FANTASY PINO: I think I was just terrified
Of how madly I loved you
You're the woman of my dreams
Whatever our souls are made of, yours and mine are the same

SHY GIRL: Or something like that

And also
I know that once I show him
What I can do
...sexually or whatever
He'll realize that I'm not

36

Some shy awkward loser
And and and
And change his mind

But how do I prove myself to him
When my vagina is in such a state of disarray?

TWILIGHT

SHY GIRL: And I guess smartphones can hear our thoughts now?
—Hi big tech—
Because as I brood
Related Instagram ads start popping up
You know like sacred sexuality girlboss accounts?
Yeah [name of audience member] I know you're into that
stuff
I can see why

I'm particularly drawn to this one ad
For a company called the 'Wyld Woman Collective'?
Wyld being spelled with a Y
I'm like... that's cool?

It appears to be some sort of
Sex therapy coaching situation
I mean their mission statement is
'Harnessing the erotic power of the divine feminine and
downloading orgasmic codes from the cosmos'

And I'm kind of like... yeah
That sounds about right
I've been foolishly searching for the answer
To my timid vagina in the material world
When this is clearly a matter to be taken up with the spiritual

So
I quickly book an appointment with a Wyld Woman sex
therapist
Named Twilight
Who I can tell is like
Enlightened
I'm pretty sure

And we get on Skype
—She's old school—
And I give her the rundown
You know
That I've met my person

—Talking about Pino obviously—
We're super into each other
But um... I can't seem to have sex with him
(Irish accent) Much less fit his wee finger within me

Twilight nods
she's seen it all before

SHY GIRL goes to the window, facing out. She caresses the curtains, becoming TWILIGHT.

TWILIGHT: Have you seen Cirque de Soleil?
By the end of our time together
That's what your pussy should feel like
Aerial silks and acrobats abound

Now the pussy
The funny thing about the pussy
Is that she has a psyche all her own
And that psyche
I want to mine its depths

Now talk to me
Who is your pussy?

Well
Is your pussy a secret garden where hummingbirds flit and fairies flutter?
Is your pussy an ancient basilica full of stained glass and virgin Marys?
Is your pussy a desert oasis where seething cacti guard your most precious watering hole?
These things you must establish dear-ling

If I did not know my pussy
If I did not adore my pussy
If I did not *worship* my pussy
Surely I couldn't fit a phallus within her confines
She wouldn't trust me
She'd erect an ivory tower
She'd guard herself with a fire-breathing dragon
And mote of lava

Even a Scottish ogre and his donkey friend couldn't access
The sacred sweetheart that is my princess vajina

SHY GIRL: "So like
What should I do?"

TWILIGHT: Well it'd do you good to shower thy pussy in
affirmations
Like so
My pussy is prophetic
My pussy is prompt
My pussy is a quarter Portuguese
—True story
My Grandmother Maria was born just outside of Lisbon—

SHY GIRL: "Oh nice!"

TWILIGHT: Now, darest thou enter with tremulous precision the
womb-like container of your transformation?

SHY GIRL: Awkward silence
Cuz I literally have no idea
What she's talking about

TWILIGHT: To put it in laywoman's terms
What makes you feel sex-sual?

SHY GIRL: What makes me feel sex-sual?
Oh God well I'd—
Well you know I mean
It's I'm not like opposed to sex, [name of audience member]
I'm just shy

But I guess in my mind
Sex feels like a... forbidden glance across a Downton Abbey
dinner table
Or salty breeze from the Mediterranean Sea (*gestures to
Imaginary Lover*)
Or or
Or a lustful strut down the streets of Paris

The Ratatouille music returns.

PARIS

SHY GIRL: Paris... Paris!
  Of course Paris makes me feel sex-sual
  I mean
  Think about me and Pino
  We work at Chez Maxence
  We love Ratatouille
  We— (*Okay, those are all the reasons. She chooses victory nonetheless*)
  Whoa
  Paris is like our thing!

  I log off Skype with a newfound determination
  I've got to see Pino ASAP
  We're gonna have bountiful sex
  And it's gonna be Paris-themed

  So I buy a sexy French outfit from the local modiste AKA
  Halloween store
  —I run into Jurgen the gynecologist there shopping for
  scrubs
  I guess that's where he gets his doctor garb?—

  And suddenly
  It's showtime again baby

  I show up to Pino's house to surprise him
  "SURPRISE!"
  I can't tell if he's excited to see me
  But I think he is
  I ask him

  "Monseiur"
  —Remember I get really shy about saying French words but
  I'll do anything for love—
  "Monsieur, would you like me to butter your baguette?"

PINO: Butter my baguette?
  Yeah
  That'd be swell

SHY GIRL: "D'accord mon cherie"

PINO: What's that about?

SHY GIRL: "Oh nothing
　　I'll just get to work"

　　And the blow job commences

　　A blowjob ballet sequence ensues, set to the song from Swan Lake. Yeah, that
　　song. This is accompanied by some pre-recorded PINO sounds of pleasure and
　　instruction. At one point, he pulls a Tar, conducting SHY GIRL with music
　　terms such as staccato and legato.

　　Her ballet is an endeavor of overwhelming effort and little grace. No move is
　　left untried. Think fouettes, pas de chats, the macarena, mime football-playing,
　　an Irish gig, the robot, etc. Mid arabesque, SHY GIRL removes her clothes to
　　reveal a "PARIS" leotard and tutu. A Ratatouille headband is donned at one
　　point. This is no quick n' easy blowjob. The music ends.

PINO: C'I come on your titties?

　　Lights shift back into post-blow job reality.

SHY GIRL: So that happens!
　　"Okay Pino let's have sex sex now"
　　I mean my inner goddess is howling for the full monty
　　Pino, unfortunately, is totally knackered

PINO: Apologies, little lady
　　But I am juiced out for the day

SHY GIRL: Awww
　　I really wanted to prove my
　　(*French accent*) sexual capabilities

　　But then I take a chill pill (*mimes taking chill pill, perhaps chokes on*
　　water)
　　And I'm like, oh blessing-in-disguise alert?
　　Cuz now I have some time to just lay around
　　And connect on a more romantic level
　　With my beloved
　　And maybe convince him that actually
　　He does want to marry me
　　Especially since he did just come on my titties

SHY GIRL lays across the dining table, looking up lovingly at the audience members sitting there.

"Pino, I really love spending time with you"

FANTASY PINO: I love spending time with you, my darling
In fact, I think I'm falling in love with you

SHY GIRL: OK yeah, [name of dining table audience member] that was fantasy Pino
But real life Pino might as well say the same thing
He goes...

PINO: I uh
I like your
Funny outfit?

SHY GIRL: Boom boom pow!
This French blow job is a huge win
For me
And my relationship with Pino

And I'm like
Who should I call to celebrate?
My first thought is Pino
But [name of audience member], you know me, I like to play hard to get
So the obvious next choice is Shelly, my therapist
She counts as a friend... Or like my best friend

I ring her up
"Hey Shelly
Is now a good time?"

SHELLY: I'm at the playground with my Mikachu and my Pikachu

SHY GIRL: That's what she calls her grandparents
She's a genius

SHELLY: But they say I can have five minutes of screen time

SHY GIRL: "OK awesome
I'll keep it quick
Um
I just had a really great date with my boyfriend"

SHELLY: Oh wee

SHY GIRL: "Yeah
And then I told him I loved spending time with him"

SHELLY: Nice sugar glider
What did he say?

SHY GIRL: "Oh...
That he likes my—my funny outfit"

SHELLY: Oh? Okay

SHY GIRL: "Yeah
I like
Love him"

SHELLY: What do you love about him?

SHY GIRL: "Sorry?"

SHELLY: What do you love about him?
I mean is he funny?
Is he sweet like cake?
Does he just really get you?

I just
I just don't know that much about him
I mean does he—

The doorbell to the apartment buzzes. SHY GIRL freezes and then panics.

SHY GIRL: Oh my God
Oh my God oh my God oh my God
They're here

She tries to put on the clothes she took off during the ballet, but can't find the right holes. Classic. She almost goes to fix the dining table, but the buzzer rings again!

Oh God!!
Okay
Act normal!

She presses a button on the buzzer and a light switch on the wall. Lights restore to the preshow look.

Opening ambience!

SHY GIRL sprints out of the apartment, running down the hall. From far away we hear her scream.

ALEXA! PLAY THEIR ENTRANCE MUSIC!!

Party music begins blasting. A few moments later, SHY GIRL returns, out of breath and holding a bag of Chipotle.

Alexa pause!
ALEXA PAUSE!!

Party music stops.

Nonsense nonsense nonsense
It was just the food I ordered for us!
I know right
I was like
I am not ready
[Audience member's name], you were literally having a panic attack
Like chill please
[Another audience member's name] you kept it cool
Thank you for grounding us

SHY GIRL eyes the chips in the Chipotle bag and reaches for one.

Ahhh
Eating in front of people
Makes me so embarrassed

She offers it to an audience member and watches as they munch.

Yeah that's pretty awkward
I love you though

SHY GIRL notices the index cards.

Oh my God!
I completely forgot about these
Umm

Where was I?
Oh

BAD DAY

SHY GIRL: Do you guys ever have bad days like I do?

...

Nice yeah

Well for me
Actually the day after
The French blow job I was just telling you about
I go out to eat at a restaurant by myself
Do you guys know Chipotle?

Light change. We're in Chipotle.

At first it's really great cuz
I mean
I get in without a reservation
Cuz I'm not with like friends or my boyfriend
I mean I'm with my imaginary friends
But they have imaginary chairs so that's no trouble

And then I order this burrito
That's like incredible
(*ordering*) "No meat for me please
I'm a virgin!"

And I'm sitting near that group of legends
From my neighborhood
Who I'm literally obsessed with
"HIIII LEGENDS"
Is what I would say if I wasn't so shy
But I'm totally eavesdropping on their conversation
Inhaling their cigarette smoke
Pretending I'm one of them
When suddenly...
Pino walks in
TO MY CHIPOTLE

47

At first I'm all giddy
Like whoa
A spontaneous date
(*to the Heavens*) Thanks, God?

But then it gets really bad
Cuz I realize...
He's with a girl

That sad song from Pixar's Up begins to play.

(*singing*) A COOL GIRL

The song from Up starts to play in my head???

Pino and the Cool Girl sit at table directly next to me
So I hide behind my burrito
But I've eaten most of it
Pino introduces me to the Cool Girl

PINO: Uh this is uh
My coworker

COOL GIRL: Nice to meet you, sweetie
Oh! You have a
Little black bean in your teeth

SHY GIRL: "Oh yeah
I put that there on purpose!"

SHY GIRL sings the following to the tune of the Up song. Terribly, but not without passion and a sort of Norah Jones huskiness.

AND I START TO CRY
NOT BECAUSE I CARE
I JUST GET REALLY EMOTIONAL WHEN–

HE'S ON A DATE
WITH A GIRL
BUT I THOUGHT HE LOVED ME

OR AT LEAST
I WAS GONNA MAKE HIM LOVE ME

ONCE I GOT SKILLED AT SEX
AND UNSHY AND THAT KINDA STUFF

I MEAN
I DON'T UNDERSTAND
LIKE WHAT
WHAT HAPPENED?

The song ends.

And then I'm like no!
Surely there's been some misunderstanding!
That's the only possible explanation

So I wipe my tears
I pluck the black bean out of my tooth
And I pull my seat up to their table

 "Pino?
Pino?
Do you like me?"

FANTASY PINO: Like you?
Darling
I love you

SHY GIRL: Ugh
Fantasy Pino again

No
Regular Pino is a little less
Emotionally available

PINO: Uh
Kind of awkward to be addressing this
While I'm on a Chipotle date
But um
No?

I thought I made that clear
When I gave you the whole
'I don't want anything serious talk' a little while back

SHY GIRL: And then this part gets a little hazy but I think he goes

PINO: Listen
You're a great...
Coworker and listener and... and stuff
But your problem is you're so quiet
I've never really connected with you

THE CACOPHONY

A low rumble. The lights begin to flicker and change.

SHY GIRL: 'Your problem is you're so quiet I've never really connected with you'
'Your problem is you're so quiet I've never really connected with you...'

SHY GIRL begins to cycle frenziedly through the people in her life as the rumble builds.

JURGEN: No your problem is
You are weird virgin who watches Ratatouille

TWILIGHT: No dearling
Your problem is you simply haven't
Thrust yourself unto the pyre of your own orgasmic knowing

MEMPHIS: No your problem is
You don't have that *je ne sais quoi* that makes a man interested

PATRICE: No your problem is
Because of you
Michael Caine
Posh Spice
and Prince Andrew
All couldn't fucking hear the soup du jour

SHELLY: Your problem is
I don't know
I'm only six

PINO: 'Your problem is you're so quiet I've never really connected with you'
'Your problem is you're so quiet I've never really connected with you'
'Your problem is you're so quiet I've never really connected with you...'
Your problem is you're so quiet I'VE NEVER REALLY CONNECTED TO YOU

The rumble cuts out. SHY GIRL looks around, disoriented.

SHY GIRL: Oh my god
I'm still at Chipotle!

Lights restore to Chipotle.

PINO: Dude you were like
Talking to yourself

SHY GIRL: Yeah...
I do that sometimes...

PINO: That's... awkward

SHY GIRL: "That's awkward"

PINO: Yeah, that's awkward

SHY GIRL: I try to think of something clever and awesome to say
To make him love me or I'd even take like me at this point
But all that comes out is

"Oh I um yeah oh uh Okay well"
You know
Like shy stuff?

SHY GIRL is ravaged. Her loserness can no longer be denied.

WYLD WOMAN

SHY GIRL: I don't sleep all night
    I toss and turn
    There's thunder and lightning

The sound of thunder and lightning.

    The world feels upside down
    I don't know right from left
    Heart from vagina

    Next day?
    I'm back at work
    Chez Maxence
    Brunch shift
    I'm so depressed
    It's not seasonal
    Purely circumstantial

    I clock in
    There's Patrice

PATRICE: Hi

SHY GIRL: (*waving*) I'm too sad to say hi back

    I go to my section
    Oh dear
    Guess who's dining at table 18?
    BLEEP
    Oh yeah
    I'm not actually allowed to say his name
    But he's a really famous British Rockstar who you definitely
    know

    I try to take his order quickly
    So I can go cry in the bathroom

    But the Rockstar really wants to make conversation?

ROCKSTAR: D'you know what?
    ...
    D'you know what?

SHY GIRL: "Oh uh… what?"

ROCKSTAR: I love dining alone like this
Sitting solo with me thoughts
Goin' real internal
Openin' up those inner rivers
So the muse can paddle in
As though me mind's a venetian canal
And me genius is a sort of gondola
D'you know what I mean

SHY GIRL: "Not really"

ROCKSTAR: Oh you don't get it

SHY GIRL: "No problem
Um it might be hard to hear this
But our special side dish today is petits pois a la francaise
David Attenborough missed out on those
Due to my quiet voice
So you'd be really lucky to have them"

ROCKSTAR: Lucky yeah?

SHY GIRL: "Yeah"

ROCKSTAR: Really lucky

SHY GIRL: "Uh huh
So do you want to order anything
Or just the check?"

ROCKSTAR: To be quite frank
I'd like to fuck you

SHY GIRL: "Sorry?"

Stunned mega pause.

ROCKSTAR: I'd like to fuck you
I think you're fit
Which is a compliment in British

SHY GIRL: What? What is happening?
I look up
There's Pino

He's wearing his retainer
He's waiting on Dame Judi Dench
Even Dame Judi can't deny his magnetism

I turn back to the Rockstar
A British man with a voice like butter
But oh dear me
I say

"I'm sorry Sir
I don't think I can do that
I was made a scorned woman at Chipotle yesterday
So my heart is shattered to smithereens"

And with that
I clock out
—short shift—
And run out of Chez Maxence
Directly into a cloud of cigarette smoke

Oh no!
It's the group of legends from my neighborhood
They can't see me like this

But they do
And they want to talk to me?

SHY GIRL sits on a stoop and smokes a cigarette, becoming the LEGENDS.

LEGENDS: Hey
Hey you

SHY GIRL: "Who? Me?"

LEGENDS: Yeah you
We're waiting out here to see if we can meet *BLEEP*
We saw you talking to him

SHY GIRL: "Oh yeah
I um... I sort of rejected him
It's not the right time"

LEGENDS: Dude
That is... badass

SHY GIRL: "What?"

LEGENDS: That is totally fuckin' badass
    You just do whatever the hell you want to do huh?

SHY GIRL: "I mean—"

LEGENDS: We also saw you have a meltdown at Chipotle yesterday
    In front of that weird guy
    That was real as fuck
    You are cool

SHY GIRL: "Oh
    ...
    Yeah
    You are too"

LEGENDS: Do you want to bum a cigarette?

SHY GIRL: "No thank you"

LEGENDS: Do you want some equestrian grade ketamine?

SHY GIRL: "No thank you either"

And then
I realize
I'm being overtaken by the courage of a thousand blazing
suns
And before I can even think
The words are coming out of my mouth
I go

"But what I do want...
What I do want...
Is to invite you guys to my house tomorrow night for a
dinner party
...
If you want to come"

And the legends go

LEGENDS: Yeah
    Yeah we do

Triumphant music plays as SHY GIRL grabs the LEGENDS by the hands and jumps with them—think that epic High School Musical jump.

ENDING

SHY GIRL: OKAY PAUSE!
That dinner party?
Happening any second
I'm like about to belong to a group of legends I'm pretty sure

And yeah, [name of audience member], I know after like
Almost losing my virginity from behind
And initiating that group hang with the Legends
I now come off as like a free spirited siren

But I still can be a little nervous and shy
So I wanted to take some time
To have you know
A practice conversation
With index card prompts that Shelly and I wrote together
—Well I wrote them cuz Shelly's still learning how to read
and write—

And test them out
On a supportive audience of
My favorite imaginary friends

OH MY GOD don't tell the other imaginary friends
That I like you guys best
Like especially Jason and Anita
They get such bad fomo
Especially after that rift with you, [name of audience
member]
Last week OMG
I was like I do not want to get in the middle of that

SHY GIRL puts cigarettes at each place setting.

Legend favors

SHY GIRL dons a beanie and fake tattoo sleeves.

Legend gear

Yeah I'm feeling ready

Like I'm just gonna tell the legends everything I told you guys

SHY GIRL hands the stack of index cards back to the audience member who held them at the beginning.

—Please make sure I stay on track—
I mean this felt so good!

SIRI: Text from: LEGEND FORGOT TO ASK HER NAME GOT TOO EXCITED SUNGLASSES EMOJI

SHY GIRL: Oh my God yay!

SIRI: "Hey biddy. Constantine had a bad trip. DMT and Kratom. We can't make your party. Hope you have fun with all your other friends."

SHY GIRL: ...

SIRI: Would you like me to repeat the message?

SHY GIRL: ...

SIRI: "Hey biddy. Constantine—"

SHY GIRL: No stop!!!
    ...

Long pause. SHY GIRL is devastated. Not just playing devastated. Devastated in real time.

Oh
    ...
Oh my God
    ...
The legends aren't coming?
But I was—
This was all for them

She references the streamers, balloons, confetti, cigarettes, and hour of essentially stand-up she just did.

I am so stupid

Why would they be coming to hang out with me
I'm not cool
I'm shy
I'm just shy

I always get my hopes up like this
Just like I thought Pino was gonna be my boyfriend
And I was about to belong to a group of legends

I mean I wasn't gonna tell them everything
I just wanted them to get to know me
And be a little vulnerable
And I could get to know them
And they could be a little vulnerable
And that would be a really beautiful birthday
But...

Oh yeah it's my birthday
But you guys know that
Of course you know that
You know everything

Pause.

You know everything

You know Memphis and I aren't actually close
I don't get her sense of humor

And you know I don't actually like working at Chez Maxence
I only do it so I can see all the British customers
But Patrice is really crazy

And you know I don't need a Divine Feminine Sex Coach
from the Internet
She's so weird
You know my pussy is not a secret garden
My pussy is not a quarter Portuguese
It's a quarter Irish, just like I am
And it'll open in due time

But that doesn't mean I have to go to a scary German
gynecologist
Why is he German? This is New York City

This is New York City and there are a lot of amazing people here
So you know it's pretty exhausting to pretend that a guy
whose name is literally Pino
Is one of the great minds of our generation
I read a sample of his manuscript
Which is literally just his journal
And it's just about how many times a day he drinks water
Which is not even that much!

So Pino has never really connected to me
Is that because I'm so quiet
Or because we have absolutely nothing in common
Seeing as I don't like reddit
And I don't wear my retainer to work
And I don't like Ratatouille

I fucking hate Ratatouille
I only like Up

Oh you guys
You're always so good to me
Like [name of audience member], you always make me laugh
And [name of audience members] you guys are so popular
but also so inclusive
[name of audience member], you sing to me every time I cry
in the bathroom
And [name of audience member], always look away when I
eat

I'm happy to be spending my birthday with you

You see me as I am you know
You know me
You really do
And when I see myself through the eyes of the people who
really know me
I see love
I just see love

—And it's not because the Legends said I was cool
Or because a famous British rockstar wants to have sex with me
Though both those things are true—

It's just that I love you and I love me
And love has set me free
And that's all I've ever wanted

I mean
I'm a romantic

'On The Street Where You Live' begins to play.

Like this is my anthem

And yeah I'm shy as fuck
And yeah my hands shake when people look at me
And yeah my most romantic memory is literally just listening
to this song

But I'm tender
And I'm funny
And I'm kind

Okay? And I don't do what I don't want to do
And I do do what I do want to do

SHELLY: You sound like a legend to me

SHY GIRL: Oh my God, Shelly?

SHELLY: Hiii-iii

SHY GIRL: Were you listening this whole time?

SHELLY: Sure was

SHY GIRL: Oh God
     I'm sorry

SHELLY: No sorries puppy cat
     You're so wonderful

SHY GIRL: Thank you
     Listen Shelly
     I should go
     I'm think I'm about to rage with my imaginary friends
     And they go kinda hard
     Especially [name of audience member]

SHELLY: That's so true

Okay
Happy Birthday!

SHY GIRL: Thanks

She hangs up the phone. Actually.

Yeah she's pretty awesome
So... You guys wanna drink Memphis' mango-flavored vodka
or what?

SIRI: Text from Legend I Forgot Her Name Got Too Excited
Sunglasses Emoji

SHY GIRL: "Oh?"

SIRI: "BTW we're all meeting for Chipotle and cigarettes
tomorrow at 7:30.
Would luv 2 c u there"

SHY GIRL: Oh my God
...
...
...

I've gotta practice what I'm going to say!

BLACKOUT

END

ALSO AVAILABLE FROM SALAMANDER STREET

All Salamander Street plays can be bought in bulk at a discount for performance or study. Contact info@ salamanderstreet.com to enquire about performance licenses.

ALGORITHMS by Sadie Clark

ISBN: 9781738429394

Brooke has it all: the job, the flat, the girlfriend but what happens when things go tits up just before your 30th birthday? A bisexual Bridget Jones for the online generation.

EAT THE RICH (but maybe not me mates x) by Jade Franks

ISBN: 9781068233449

A sharp, funny look at class, identity and friendship. Jade Franks's solo show asks "What happens when a Liverpool girl crashes the Cambridge bubble?"

CARA AND KELLY ARE BEST FREINDS FOREVER FOR LIFE by Mojola Akinyemi

ISBN: 9781068233418

A darkly comic two-hander that exposes the nastiest sides of teenage girlhood.

COWBOYS AND LESBIANS by Billie Esplen

ISBN: 9781914228902

A queer romantic comedy that examines the intersection between sexuality and fantasy through the eyes of two closeted teenage girls, highlighting just how much the stories we consume affect the ones we tell about ourselves..

LITTLE WIMMIN by Figs In Wigs

ISBN: 9781913630065

The Figs turn the classic novel on its head before dismantling it entirely and transforming it into an unrecognisable cosmic catastrophe that talks about climate change, astrology and the infinite nature of the universe. PS: Beth Dies.

Salamander Street